STOP THE SPREAD

PUBLIC LIES....PRIVATE TRUTHS

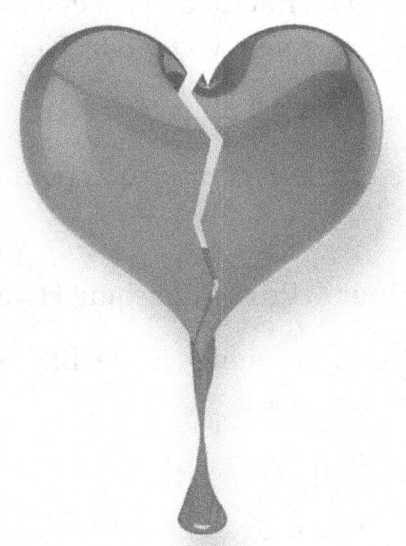

ALFREDA COLEMAN

Copyright © 2021 Alfreda Coleman

ALL RIGHTS RESERVED. This book contains material protected under International and Federal Copyright Laws and Treaties. Any unauthorized reprint or use of this material is prohibited. No part of this book may be reproduced or transmitted in any form or by any means, electronic or mechanical, including photocopying, recording, or by any information storage and retrieval system without express written permission from the author/publisher.

Unless otherwise noted, all Scripture quotations are taken from the New International Version of the Bible. All rights reserved. www.BibleGateway.com.

Used by permission. All rights reserved.

All definitions are derived from Merriam-Webster Dictionary

Book Cover Design: Prize Publishing House

Printed by: Prize Publishing House, LLC in the United States of America.

First printing edition 2021.

Prize Publishing House
P.O. Box 9856, Chesapeake, VA 23321

www.PrizePublishingHouse.com

ISBN (Paperback): 978-1-7374791-1-6

ISBN (E-Book): 978-1-7374791-2-3

"The thief enters only to steal and kill and destroy; I have come that they may have life and have it to the full."

John 10:10 (NIV)

ENDORSEMENTS

Although the lessons within the following pages are concise and brief, they were not learned quickly. The truths in these lessons tendered to the mind will change your life if engendered in the heart. A friend once told me the preacher A.W. Tozer taught above her head, but the reality was that he was speaking into her heart, and the flesh resists corrective truth. It also resists the slough of self-satisfaction. Alfreda Coleman's lessons are not over the head but are liberating truths that will cut into your heart if you give place to the Sword of the Spirit.

Robert Dennis
Easley, South Carolina

Stop the Spread is a remedy that addresses the emotional and mental elephants in the room of our souls. It is a Godsend, written in such a way that matures us in love, catapults us to wholeness, and helps us get rooted in the freedom Christ died for.

Pastor Angie Cleveland
Faith to Faith Glory to Glory Ministries
Spartanburg, South Carolina

CONTENTS

FOREWORD 1
ACKNOWLEDGEMENTS 2
INTRODUCTION 4
IDENTIFY YOUR NEMESIS 7
THAT'S JUST THE WAY I AM 11
THE SILENT KILLER 15
THE PARASITIC 20
THE MIRROR 25
YOUR MIND ACCOUNT 30
MOTIVES 35
PUBLIC LIES, PRIVATE TRUTHS 39
THE EMERGENCE 43
PRAYER OF SALVATION 48
PRAYER OF VICTORY 49
REFERENCES 50

FOREWORD

Serving as the Chief Executive Officer of GENUINELY ZOE, an effective, productive portal to provide women from all walks of life tools for overall health and wellness, Alfreda Coleman certifies to bring to the forefront an awareness of gathered information to help better ourselves through this devotional, *STOP THE SPREAD*. To IDENTIFY OUR NEMESIS sets us forth to the EMERGENCE of our best God-created self.

These chapters carry you on a journey of consideration that is sure to be challenging, provoking, encouraging, and catapulting into healing, wholeness, and well-being! *STOP THE SPREAD* is truly a timely writing!

Pastor T. Renea Glenn
Lead Pastor of Restoration Church of Prayer
Wellford, South Carolina

ACKNOWLEDGEMENTS

To God Be All the Glory, Honor, and Power for my Sufficiency is in Him Alone!

As I ponder the acknowledgments for this devotional, my mind goes in many directions. God has been kind and gracious to me by blessing my life with some pretty amazing people. I first want to thank God for my mother, Jessie Wells Phelps. I was privileged to serve her in the last years of her life. One of the most impactful, as there were many, statements she made to me was, "Let no one talk you out of having a better life, including you." Thank you, Mom, for your prayers are still working in my life.

To my husband, my dude, and best friend, Charles, God has truly been good to us. We have come through the best and the worst of times, and we are still here by His Grace. Thank you for covering me in prayer, encouraging me in all my endeavors, and bringing constant joy to my life. I appreciate you more than you know, and I am grateful and honored to be your wife. I Love You!

To my children, grands, and family beyond, you all mean the world to me, and I am grateful for your love and support!

To my pastor, counselor, spiritual mother, and more, Pastor T. R. Glenn, I do not have adequate words to ascribe to you what you mean to me. Thank you for your counsel, correction, instruction, and affirmation. You patiently challenge me and diligently pray that I become who God ordained in the earth. I truly honor, respect, and love you!

To the many men and women of God who have loved and encouraged me on this journey, you all have truly impacted, motivated, and blessed me in ways I cannot count. Thank You for your labor of love toward me. I honor you all!

To the women of Genuinely ZOE, you have embraced me, and we are continually growing, maturing, and valuing others unconditionally. Thank you for trusting me with your stories and challenging and encouraging me along the way. We have made strides together, and I am honored to know each of you. Let's keep growing and **celebrating each other as we pursue ZOE, the God Kind of Life!**

INTRODUCTION

"Wow" is the word that comes to mind as we admittedly recognize that this pandemic is much deeper than COVID-19. Interestingly, as much as we have all been forced to drastically change the dynamic of our interactions, it has been a most rewarding season if we allowed our perspectives to release what we have called 'normal.' Frankly, I am not so sure that we were ever normal, so maybe this time has been instrumental in setting us into what life was supposed to look like. But I am not here to talk about that; the reason I am writing this short devotional is to take an introspective look at the inward spread of a silent killer called Dysfunction. We can rename it to sound a little more socially acceptable; however, we are going to stick with the deep raw truths that we have conveniently disguised.

What does that have to do with public lies and private truths? Glad you asked! For many years I did a lot of work to maintain an image my private life did not undergird. Sure, I did the expected for the most part, but one of the most essential keys needed to live a healthy and whole life was not consistently present; the key component of honesty. Now, before you think this should be the norm in the life of a believer, you're right. But the truth is, sometimes, that is not the case. It does not matter how wonderful we sing, teach, run a business, serve in the local assembly or in your home;

if we are not taking time to address our hostile private truths, we will slowly become intoxicated with the wine of accolades, platforms, and name connections in public. The lie we know deep within will become the lie we live out loud. There is absolutely no room for dysfunction in the life of a Believer. You cannot silence dysfunction; it demands all or nothing. You cannot tame or calm it, for it will spread at will. After all, that's what it was designed to do as an agent of the enemy of our soul.

To annihilate the spread of dysfunction, it takes more than a ritualistic declaration. When we take a deep look at the triggers and foundational behavior without taking the time to stop the internal bleeding, it silently kills our purpose, our relationships, and every other aspect of our lives. As we journey through a few areas of dysfunction, it will surely reveal others; this is a good thing. Take advantage of the note section provided after each chapter to assist you on your journey. Be brutally honest with yourself, with God, expose the secrets, dysfunctions, and negativity; write it down. Give yourself the kindness and respect to start the journey; do this for YOU! Holy Spirit is committed to our healing, deliverance, and well-being. I have already prayed for us, and we will become whole, healthy, and well, day by day. Together, with the help of the Holy Spirit, we say that the spread of dysfunction stops NOW!

TAKE A BREATH AND LET'S GET STARTED!

Use the points below as you journal after each chapter.

- What did you recognize about yourself in this chapter? (Name everything, big or small)

- Be specific in the areas you are bringing to the Lord.

- Search scriptures pertaining to your area of need.

- Pray with honesty to the Father in confession.

- Forgive yourself!

- Receive His forgiveness and cleansing.

For your consideration: Find a person who can serve as an accountability partner (someone you esteem as safe and honorable) and share your journey. A few ideas of an accountability partner would be a pastor, family member, or friend. This can help facilitate your healing and fortify your wins!

IDENTIFY YOUR NEMESIS

The word nemesis is defined as a downfall caused by an inescapable agent ("Nemesis"). It's interesting how the cause of a downfall is noted as something you cannot escape. For many years of my life, I allowed triggers and self-sabotage to control my narratives which essentially made me feel like a jailed bird with the door open. It seems logical that if a door is made available, you simply exit, but not when you believe it is safer to stay in the cage. A study on birds recently noted that birds are highly reactive, and if they see a way out, they will take it. The exception would be the bird that has adapted to being secluded or alone. For this bird, the mere thought of leaving the familiar area and venturing out into the unknown would cause delirium (confused thinking or reduced awareness).

Before you say, "that could never be me," know that when dysfunction goes unaddressed, you will find yourself doing the very thing you said you never would do. You become so accustomed to the twisted environment that is killing you that the thought of venturing out into the unknown is not an option. Though our triggers are likened to Russian roulette, which eventually destroys us, it often appears better to live with the known nemesis than to cross the threshold of unknown freedom.

The way to escape or incapacitate this enemy is through the Word of God and prayer. Let's face it –

introspection looks messy, and identifying the very thing that nourishes dysfunction feels dangerous. The truth is that when you decide to go deep, that is the best way to sever the root that feeds your nemesis. You must call it what it is: rejection, low self-esteem, jealousy, envy, offense, anger, etc. It all has a growth center that nourishes the inner core of our identity.

You may be thinking, "This has become part of my identity, so how can I sever what has comforted me for so long?" Again, if you do not address the thing that has controlled your life, you will not escape its grip, it will always randomly surface, and it will manipulate your life. Let us take the first step of honestly acknowledging and confessing that it is time to uproot everything that nourishes unhealthy patterns and dysfunction. Do not shrink back because of embarrassment or shame. Remember, the Word of God has the answer, and Holy Spirit is already present waiting on you. He is madly in love with you, and trust me, there is absolutely nothing that can take Him by surprise. In fact, He already knows! Let's dig and uproot!

Scripture: "Therefore, there is now no condemnation [no guilty verdict, no punishment] for those who are in Christ Jesus [who believe in Him as personal Lord and Savior]. For the law of the Spirit of life [which is] in Christ Jesus [the law of our new being] has set you free from the law of sin and of death." Romans 8:1-2 (AMP)

Stop the Spread – Alfreda Coleman

NOTES OF HONESTY

Take a moment and name the triggers that have ensnared your life. Call it what it is!

_____

_____

_____

_____

_____

_____

_____

_____

_____

_____

_____

_____

_____

_____

_____

_____

_____

_____

Stop the Spread – Alfreda Coleman

THAT'S JUST THE WAY I AM

Have you ever used the phrase, "That's just the way I am"? We probably have said it without realizing its implications. When we make this statement, it becomes not only a message to the hearer but also a signal to the enemy of our soul that we agree with the fact that our behaviors, actions, and lives are not up for debate nor change. When we add our agreement to these words by speaking to them, they create and refute any opposition or correction presented.

In the previous chapter, we discussed identifying our nemesis. If we choose not to take this step, we will remain just as we are, and what a tragedy it is to oppose growth and maturity, which we were all created to do. We have all been given the privilege of decision, and whatever we choose, we become a slave to. To be a slave to your dysfunction means you have given up your freedom of choice. Dysfunctions, unhealthy behaviors, and systems will only take you deeper into the trap of "that's just the way I am." Ultimately, this seduction is guided by the enemy of our soul.

As stated, every day, we are created to grow and mature. The challenge starts when you feel as if you have reached some pinnacle of importance or maxed out on knowledge and refuse to continue evolving into who God has created you to be. So, to make such statements would be to employ arrogance and pride, which the Lord hates. The next time you feel yourself tensing up when your words contradict your behavior, take a breath and choose to be open to releasing the pseudo version you have created. Realize that when you say, "this is just the way I am," you are admitting that you have allowed yourself to be entrapped in a less than beggarly life. Whew, sounds rough, doesn't it? But the act of confronting lies and accepting the truth is designed to free you from the imposter. It is a known fact we are not here on our own, and we need the Father's help to BE who He says we are and not who we have created ourselves to be. Let us go deeper!

The Father is looking for the 'New Creation' in the earth!

Scriptures:

- "Therefore, if anyone is in Christ, he is a new creation; old things have passed away; behold, all things have become new." 2 Corinthians 5:17 (KJV)

- "And those who belong to Christ Jesus have crucified the sinful nature together with its passions and appetites." Galatians 5:24 (AMP)

NOTES OF HONESTY

Think about the negative areas of your life you have excused and expected others to accept without question.

Stop the Spread – Alfreda Coleman

THE SILENT KILLER

Have you ever felt like you had so much to say but could not muster enough strength to say it? Then, when you finally do open your mouth, you feel so minimized that you intentionally cut yourself off. Being alive and having no voice is more common than you think. Believe it or not, this often leads to a life of secrecy, which is a covert weapon used against the believer that we express as stubbornness, selfishness, and sometimes retaliation.

Let's face it, we know when we need help, deliverance, or guidance, but all of these characteristics will speak loudly to us, building a front to refute sound counsel. Yeah, I am talking about the committee in your head that feeds you the lie that everyone is against you, or it's just better to remain muted, especially when the truth is present. It is imperative that you are honest with yourself and others. If you ever feel like you can't voice your true feelings, suppressing thoughts and emotions can easily turn on you and become traumatizing. Your misery, trouble, and regret can and will silently counsel you, and it has no intention of you being well. This is a silent killer!

We all need a safe space to release our innermost thoughts, pain, and concerns. The enemies of our souls will fight us on every side to prevent this type of release as he is totally against it! There are a few reasons why many feel as if they would never allow themselves to be vulnerable in this area: past infractions and the sin of offense. I tell you, this culprit has destroyed many people and ordained relationships since the beginning of time.

Eve chose to be offended in the garden. Remember how the enemy told her that if God knew she'd eaten of the tree, she would be just like Him? What was that other than a trick to make her feel that God really did not want the best for her and divert her from the truth?

Offense happens when we feel disregarded or insulted; one of its main motives is to cause us to withdraw and snarl at accountability. We are much more likely to compromise when it seems like no one cares about what we are doing or thinking. Offense is the bait of Satan, and if not confronted, it will betray you and possibly influence you to betray your offender as a form of revenge. Hence, we must uproot this Spirit.

With that, accountability is so important. Just as your voice is important and should never be dismissed, you should always give that same space to others. Accountability can be challenging but rewarding if we are willing to take responsibility for our actions.

It is important to establish a safe place to process, which you may already have. If that is the case, ask Holy Spirit to help you with the decision to step into freedom by using your voice to communicate and seek understanding. Today, let's expose the Silent Killer by removing the fear of using our authentic voice to pave the way to true freedom! There is absolutely NO secret that God will hold against you. Allow yourself to be vulnerable before Him so that He can build you up again. He is so in love with you!

Scripture: "And ye shall know the truth, and the truth shall make you free." John 8:32 (KJV)

Stop the Spread – Alfreda Coleman

NOTES OF HONESTY

What offense(s) has silenced you? Write/talk it out!

_____
_____
_____
_____
_____
_____
_____
_____
_____
_____
_____
_____
_____
_____

Stop the Spread – Alfreda Coleman

THE PARASITIC

Many years ago, I recall reading an article regarding conjoined twins. One of the twins was parasitic, meaning he stopped developing and was literally draining life from the healthy twin. The stronger twin became responsible for sustaining the parasitic, thereby causing harm to himself because of their connection. After all, they grew and developed together inside the womb with hopes of living outside of the womb together.

Parasitics can be compared to toxic relationships. In our effort to stop the spread of dysfunction and unhealthy behaviors, it is imperative to take inventory of those with whom we are connected. I wholeheartedly believe that God ordains relationships, but somewhere along the way in life, circumstances, stubbornness, toxicity, and soul ties often become the nourishment of the connection.

When relationships are respected and productive, God is glorified. Of course, they require work to maintain, and when it becomes clear that only one of you is doing the fighting, the relationship can become parasitic. Whether you are a parasitic or attached to one, it slowly and covertly drains you of your value, esteem, and self-worth internally, which will soon reflect externally in every facet of your life.

Back to the article of the parasitic. When I saw the healthy twin, it was apparent that there was anguish and stress; I could only imagine how a connection between two twins could be so loving and yet so destructive at such an early stage of life. It was a soul tie to pain instead of a healthy connection to life. There is a big lesson here. Sometimes, as much as we love some folks, we must disconnect for our own well-being and theirs so that we do not enable each other's dysfunctions. I know it sounds harsh, but you may fare better disconnecting and recovering so that you may pray more effectively for them. Remember, parasitics are toxic, and their only goal is to poison purpose, assignments, relationships, and eventually life in totality. We must decide every day to choose the life outlined for us in the Word of God.

Please know that this is spiritual, and we are not here for the blame game of any person. The root of the issue is the spirit of the devil, whose primary goal is to destroy you internally, which affects your life externally. Therefore, we are taking the time to evaluate and adjust. Time is of the essence, and we need to be healthy and connected to others who have made the same decision.

Scriptures:

- *"For, brethren, ye have been called unto liberty; only use not liberty for an occasion to the flesh, but by love serve one another." Galatians 5:13 (KJV)*

- *"Can two walk together, except they be agreed?" Amos 3:3 (KJV)*

NOTES OF HONESTY

Some relationships are simply not healthy nor beneficial to your soul. Pinpoint the disruptions.

Stop the Spread – Alfreda Coleman

THE MIRROR

The mirror reflects what it sees, right? So how do we see what is in the mirror and walk away with another conclusion about what is right in front of us? It becomes easy to disregard the reflection because of excuses, self-deception, and distortion of facts that lead our lives. Is anybody honest enough to admit this? We groom ourselves to perfection when preparing to go out, yet constantly find ourselves referring back to the mirror, questioning or forgetting what we have just seen.

So it is when reading and even hearing the Word of God. We rejoice, sing, celebrate our victory, and as soon as we are out the door, we have totally forgotten that we just celebrated freedom. Do we really trust what we see in the Word of God, which is our mirror? When I look in the mirror to check my appearance, I walk away with a sense of confidence that I believe what I just beheld. How much more trust should I have when I open the Word of God? Do we check the reflection more than once, or have we become so casual that we trust the preconceived images we have accepted?

Let us not confuse positive affirmations with allowing the Word to show us what we are not. It's great to affirm ourselves, but it's even greater when we are honest about where we are, do the work and declare it.

The frustration comes when we try to affirm a lie; it may sound good saying it, but living it becomes the task. So, what is the remedy? Trust the Mirror, the Word of God.

I can remember the old tale of the queen who trusted her mirror to speak the truth every time she asked a question. It went something like this, "Mirror, mirror on the wall, who is the fairest of them all?" The mirror always affirmed her until it no longer was true. And because she did not like the answer, she became enraged and vindictive. The right response would have been to ask the mirror, "What can I do to be better?" Think about it. After all, isn't that what the mirror is designed to do – show you what it sees?

Today, if we ask the Mirror any question, it will provide the true answer, not for us to be embarrassed, angry, or belittled, but to help us come to the truth about who and where we are. The goal is for God's freedom to become our truth. I recently saw a statement that said, "When people show you who they are, believe them." I say this, when the word of God shows you who you are, believe it! Let us remove the need to confirm what we think we see and know about others and focus on what the Word of God says about us. Doing this work may assist the ones seen as fake or phony in being delivered through a life of consistent growth in character lived in front of them. The power of the Mirror, the Word of God, is what we should desire to see, and I believe we will! This is our declaration backed with obedience!

Just a reminder that Father wants you well!

Scripture: "For if anyone only listens to the word without obeying it, he is like a man who looks very carefully at his natural face in a mirror; for once he has looked at himself and gone away, he immediately forgets what he looked like." James 1:23-24 (AMP)

NOTES OF HONESTY

As you read the Word of God (the Mirror), be willing to accept the love and correction the Holy Spirit reveals. Capture your thoughts in the space below. Write scriptures that apply.

_____
_____
_____
_____
_____
_____
_____
_____
_____
_____
_____
_____
_____
_____

Stop the Spread – Alfreda Coleman

YOUR MIND ACCOUNT

Years ago, I heard a commercial stating that a mind is a terrible thing to waste. Although they were referring to education, it really made me ask myself, "Am I wasting my own mind?" It is noticeably clear that the human mind is one of the most unique parts of the human body; it can be beautiful, ugly, dangerous, and brilliant all at the same time. Everything in our mind has received some type of permission to reside.

Think about it this way – we all can pretty much say we have a bank account. There are several types of accounts to best fit our needs. Generally, the account is set up with a few perks, such as cashback or interest-bearing; the fact remains that it is designed to hold your money until you need or want it. Think of your mind as an account. What you deposit will increase as you add to it, or it will decrease as you withdraw. What are you allowing to be deposited into your account, and who have you given this precious access to?

Whatever you listen to can shape your ideas and decisions. Whatever you set your sights on will give you permission and courage to act it out. It is all in the mind. A famous quote states, "If you can conceive it, you can achieve it." Good or bad; legal or illegal; obedient or disobedient. If the enemy of our soul can woo us into believing God will look over or excuse it because of His love for us, we will do it without reservation. What we set our mind to is just that powerful!

At the onset of the pandemic in 2020, my pastor, Pastor T. R. Glenn, made a statement, "You need to determine whose voice you are going to listen to." You may be asking, *what does this have to do with the mind*? Everything! We are inundated with the news, social media, and conversation, all of which have the potential to shape our decisions, thoughts, and destiny. This can be quite overwhelming, and if not careful, we can easily become devoted to everything but the eternal state of our souls.

If you recall, in the introduction, I mentioned that we must bring attention to our core behaviors; what is driving unhealthy thoughts, addictions, toxicity, laziness, and self-sabotage? Do we understand that these behaviors draw negative interest? Do we realize that every time we reject the truth of God's Word, we fortify these negative behaviors, and they will eventually turn on us? A lot of questions that require honest answers, right? I believe this information will touch whatever negativity is present in you. The beauty is that Holy Spirit is right here now, ready to help you address it all. He is kind, gentle and all He has to give is Truth. Take some time to quiet yourself, write it all down, and give it to Him.

Let the word of Truth, God's Word, be deposited into your heart. No longer will we be a depository of empty and vile information designed to taint our minds. Father is waiting to fill us to overflow with His mind, His will, and His perfect plan.

Just a reminder that the Father wants you well!

Scripture: "Let this mind be in you, which was also in Christ Jesus." Philippians 2:5 (KJV)

Stop the Spread – Alfreda Coleman

NOTES OF HONESTY

Determine what the daily deposits in your mind consist of and make a list. What actions will you take to realign your thoughts to create positive outcomes?

_____

_____

_____

_____

_____

_____

_____

_____

_____

_____

_____

_____

_____

_____

_____

_____

_____

_____

Stop the Spread – Alfreda Coleman

MOTIVES

Have you ever felt like you were destined to save some folks? It was as if you were the only one who could rescue a family member or friend. It's not uncommon to want the best for others and even compromise yourself in doing so, but the realization is that we cannot save anyone. Only Jesus Saves.

Experience has taught me some hard lessons. One is that my focus has often been deluded by seeing the shortcomings of others and avoiding the big issue within myself. We have to be very careful that our intentions and motives are not stimulated by attention deficit or even the need to be needed. All of this can stem from failed expectations of people, acceptance, and even regret. Remember that the spread of anything negative does not stop but rather mutates into bigger issues such as control, selfishness, bad attitudes, and the list goes on.

Now, let's remove the bullet from the gun. When someone releases the truth of God's Word, it is often not them trying to run your life, but rather to assist you on your journey. In many cases, their agenda is simply wanting to see you well and walking in the truth of God's Word. However, this act of speaking into people's lives can become deadly when motives and desire for accolades infiltrate the message. The question to ask yourself is, what is your why?

Take a brutally honest moment and think of the many times you have thrown yourself into the position of being disappointed and hurt because you were trying to save someone for your fulfillment and not solely for them. One definition of motive is incentive ("Motive"). If doing what you do is to gain a footing in someone's life, which is control, you have taken on a position that will not end well. Now is the time to step back, ask the Father to search motives, and respond to whatever He reveals by admitting to it and repenting. The work part is that I learn to resist the need to be needed by the Power of God, step back and allow Jesus to do the work. Whatever void is present in your life will not be fulfilled by controlling other people and situations; trust God to be enough to give you everything you need to be whole and healthy. After all, you were not created for them. You were uniquely created for His glory alone!

Just a reminder that the Father wants you well!

Scriptures:

- *"Let no one seek [only] his own good, but [also] that of the other person." 1 Corinthians 10:24 (AMP)*

- *"Whatever you may do, do all for the honor and glory of God." 1 Corinthians 10:31b (KJV)*

Stop the Spread – Alfreda Coleman

NOTES OF HONESTY

What drives your behavior? Take a moment to examine. Is everything you do with healthy intentions? Write it down!

_____
_____
_____
_____
_____
_____
_____
_____
_____
_____
_____
_____
_____
_____
_____
_____

Stop the Spread – Alfreda Coleman

PUBLIC LIES, PRIVATE TRUTHS

Before we close with the last chapter, it is important that we take time to introspectively examine our true intent for why we do the things we do, act the way we act, and actively live our lives every day. Presentations to the world can only last so long if not founded on the truth of God's Word.

It is a fact that my private life determines what will be present to the public. Although our "public platforms" may consist of 10 or 1,000, the impact is just as heavy. Whatever you have read in this devotional and identified with, please do not excuse it or justify with your own reasoning. The litmus test is the Word of God. Whether it be a life you have led for years or experienced for a short period of time, you do not want to go another day juggling audiences as you sustain your private life of deceit.

Our loving Father is always open to our sincere cries. This is the time to bear it all to Him. I love the fact that even in the worst situation I have created or even been placed in, He is willing to listen and deliver me from any and everything; shame, regret, pain, unforgiveness; trust me, I can give you a long list. Even if I did not name your situation, all the same, Father loves you and eagerly desires the best for our lives. We are not these things listed above. As a matter of fact, we are highly valued by the Father.

Please take time to address every secret lie you have fought so hard to keep hidden. Give it all to Jesus. Leave no stone unturned! Let the tears flow. Refuse to take alternate routes of blame; this is all about you and the Father. There is absolutely nothing that can keep our Heavenly Father from receiving, healing, and delivering you. This is the one time to be focused totally on your journey to walking in Truth and Wellness.

We are in agreement with you! We declare we will no longer fight to hide from the brilliance and authenticity of who God created us to be. We are honest and truthful with ourselves as Holy Spirit is our help. Our private life of honesty and submission to the will of God undergirds our public life into one of wholeness unto the Glory of God! Let's Emerge!

LET'S TAKE ACTION!

Stop the Spread – Alfreda Coleman

THE EMERGENCE

It is time to Emerge! The word "emergence" is defined as the act of becoming into view (visible), a beginning, to launch or kickoff ("Emergence"). If we were to look at this from a natural perspective, it could be the emergence of the vaccine during the pandemic or an answer to the spread of a deadly disease. However, our focus is you and I shedding the pseudo versions of ourselves that we thought the world wanted to see and the ones we conformed to, fully emerging into the most authentic version of ourselves!

When we receive the Word of God, we are continually becoming all that God created as we experience new beginnings. Our lives were never created to remain stationary. We are uniquely wired to grow and mature constantly. Suppose we commit to stopping the spread of the many areas noted in this devotional and others. In that case, there is no reason why we will not always be on the brink of becoming all of who God created us to be, relentlessly going deeper and higher in Christ. It has been often said, "Good is the enemy of great." I believe this to be true because even when I reach the peak of growth, there will always be a greater dimension to navigate into.

Want to stop the spread of limitations? This one does not require a company to create a vaccine; this spread can be annihilated by the power of God as we believe and receive His Truth.

The emergence is you not only believing in the Word of God but also believing in the power of His Word. It's about believing in yourself, the one who God uniquely created to not only survive but to thrive every day! Do not allow fear to lock you into a limited space that will keep you confined to certain systems and cultures. The Bible is clear in 2 *Timothy 1:7, "God has not given us the spirit of fear; but of power, love and a sound mind." KJV* Fear is debilitating and will strip you of your power, love, and stability of mind. It will not allow you to increase and expand in the things God has already set forth in your life. I have to believe that it is the will and heart of God that we rise above everything that comes to hinder and interrupt what He placed in motion before the foundation of the world.

This spread can stop with you! Love and respect the beautiful person you were created to be; full of love, brilliance, creativity, and so much more. It is not too late to make necessary changes that produce health and wellness for ourselves and all connected to us.

We must believe and know that the sky is not the limit. Skyscrapers are not too tall, and oceans are not too wide. We are created to live in the overflow God has ordained for our lives in full purpose. I believe you will be a part of stopping the spread, first by doing the work in your own life. No more double lives, no more hypocrisy, no more pseudo images, no more deceit, no more pride. No More! Let's stop this spread! We have already won, and we will live like winners! Not only for ourselves but for generations to come! The emergence is in full motion! It's your time to make a decision. Don't miss it!

Just a reminder that future generations and yourself are counting on you to become well in Jesus' Name!

Scriptures:

- "It was for this freedom Christ set us free [completely liberating us]; therefore keep standing firm and do not be subject again to a yoke of slavery [which you once removed]." Galatians 5:1 (AMP)

- "But the people who do know their God shall be strong and do exploits." Daniel 11:32b (KJV)

- "These who have turned the world upside down have come here too." Acts 17:6b (KJV)

Write statements of affirmation to fortify who God says you are. Do not be afraid to agree with what the Word of God has spoken over your life!!

_____

_____

_____

_____

_____

_____

_____

_____

_____

_____

_____

_____

_____

_____

_____

_____

Stop the Spread – Alfreda Coleman

PRAYER OF SALVATION

If you have not accepted Jesus Christ as your Lord and Savior or if your relationship with him is no longer a priority, please pray this prayer with me.

Dear Lord, I acknowledge that I need you. I repent of my sin, which means to change my mind by turning to You. I ask You, Lord Jesus, to forgive me of my sins and come into my heart. I believe that You died on the cross for ME, and You rose again for ME. I believe that Your blood washes and cleanses me from all unrighteousness. I welcome Holy Spirit to lead me on my new path of freedom in Christ Jesus. Thank You for saving and restoring me!

Scriptures:

If you declare with your mouth, "Jesus is Lord," and believe in your heart that God raised him from the dead, you will be saved. Romans 10:9 (NIV)

If we confess our sins, he is faithful and just and will forgive us our sins and purify us from all unrighteousness. 1 John 1:9 (NIV)

PRAYER OF VICTORY

Father, this feels hard, but I refuse to allow what has held me hostage for so long to continue harassing and defeating me. I welcome You, Holy Spirit. I give myself totally to You. No more sabotage, no more being held hostage to my present or past, and no more being held back from the freedom You have had for me all along. Fill me with everything that is You. I trust You to help me walk this journey out in victory, in Jesus' Name!

Scriptures:

But thanks be to God! He gives us the victory through our Lord Jesus Christ. 1 Corinthians 15:57 (NIV)

You, dear children, are from God and have overcome them, because the one who is in you is greater than the one who is in the world. 1 John 4:4 (NIV)

REFERENCES

"Emergence." Merriam-Webster's Dictionary, Merriam-Webster. https://www.merriam-webster.com/dictionary/emergence. Accessed 7 July 2021

"Motive." Merriam-Webster's Dictionary,

Merriam-Webster. https://www.merriam-webster.com/dictionary/motive. Accessed 5 July 2021.

"Nemesis." Merriam-Webster's Dictionary, Merriam-Webster. https://www.merriam-webster.com/dictionary/nemesis. Accessed 5 July 2021.

www.ingramcontent.com/pod-product-compliance
Lightning Source LLC
Chambersburg PA
CBHW070051120526
44589CB00034B/1928